Contents

D1423920

Preface

This book attempts to provide an account of how mobile libraries have become part of the modern public library picture. In order to provide a satisfactory introduction to the advent of mobile libraries I have included a short account of the development of libraries in the United Kingdom so that the innovators who made the earliest attempts at book mobility will not be forgotten.

Mobile libraries as we know them today were not introduced until the early nineteen thirties and did not become an established part of the public library service until the late nineteen forties. But for the previous two centuries book availability had been advocated through circulating and travelling libraries. Within this work I have included something of the major developments in circulating and travelling library innovation.

The foundations of mobile library services were laid through the introduction of a motorised library transport system during the first thirty years of this century. Wherever possible I have commented on the major developments of motorised library transport.

This book does not purport to be a scholarly work but, I hope, a readable account of the development of mobile libraries within the public library service.

District Library Headquarters,   Ian Orton
Helenslea Road,
Dumbarton,
Strathclyde.
September, 1979.

Acknowledgements

No book is ever produced through the actions of one person and this work is certainly no exception. My thanks for all the help and advice I received, but particularly from: Mr. W. Davies of Bradford who enjoyed looking into the early travelling libraries of Bradford, Mr. K. Carter of Dorset for invaluable information on Herefordshire's first mobile library. Mr. K. King of Manchester for obtaining photographs of Manchester's first mobile library, Mr. P. Labdon of Suffolk for details of the introduction of West Suffolk's first mobile library. Mr. P. Turner of Derbyshire for details of container libraries in that County. Mr. A. Jeffress for information and a photograph of Perthshire's 1921 bookvan, Mr. D. Mortlock of Norfolk for information on the use of L.P.G. in his County. Mr. D. Donaldson of Dumfries and Galloway for a photograph of Scotland's first mobile library, Mr. G. Fletcher of Cleveland for information and photographs of Hartlepool's mobile library, Mr. L. Feiweles for a rare photograph of B. Oliph Smith, Mr. Dean Harrison for allowing reproduction of photographs of early Kent mobiles, Mr. B. Langton for information about Essex mobile libraries, Mr. J. Lendon for photographs and information about Solihull mobile libraries, Mr. F. Hallworth for allowing reproduction of photographs of the original Wiltshire County Library H.Q. and the first Wiltshire Holiday mobile. Mr. E. Porteous for identifying mobile library photographs, Mr. M. Broom for information about Hertfordshire mobile libraries, Mr. G. Smith for photographic help with Leicestershire mobile libraries, Mr. F. Green for allowing reproduction of the first West Ham mobile library, Mr. M. Messenger of Gloucestershire for allowing reproduction and supplying a photograph of Gloucestershire mobiles.

Mr. A. Edwards for information about Dyfed mobile libraries, Mr. S. Dean of Durham for permission to reproduce a photograph of Durham County mobile, Mr. A. Longworth of Lancashire, Mr. A. R. Fulton of the Scottish A.A.L. Mr. J. N.

Taylor of Nottinghamshire, the United Society for the Propagation of the Gospel, the Carnegie United Kingdom Trust for supplying essential information on early county library developments, and all mobile library contractors, but particularly G. C. Smith and Don Gresswell for going out of their way to be helpful. Additional thanks to Mr. F. A. Foster for carrying out photographic work, Miss L. V. Paulin, Miss O. S. Newman, Mr. R. Lawson, Mr. K. Stockham, Professor T. Kelly and Mr. R. Eastwood for reading through sections of the work and making helpful suggestions.

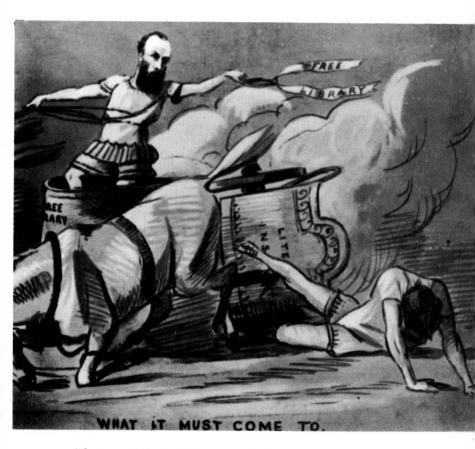

The power of the Free Library over the Literary Institutes

6

1. Mobile Libraries: The Early Years

Today the mobile library is probably the best advertisement for the public library service. Operated by all but a handful of library authorities, mobile libraries are in the front line of providing a service to all parts of the country. Attempts to supply books to isolated parts of the country have been carried out for centuries but only the advent of the internal combustion engine made such ventures possible. It is worth considering how a library service developed and how mobile libraries emerged as part of it.

During the first half of the nineteenth century pressures were building towards parliamentary approval for a free public library service. A House of Commons Select Committee under the Chairmanship of William Ewart, M.P., was set up in 1849 to find:

"the best means of extending the establishment of libraries freely open to the public especially in large towns in Great Britain and Ireland."

The Committee called a number of witnesses to familiarise itself with the state of British libraries. The first and most important witness called was Edward Edwards, then a supernumerary cataloguer assistant at the British Museum and later first Chief Librarian of Manchester. During the Committee's first meeting Edwards answered almost 300 questions. His evidence was designed to emphasise the lack of public libraries and to show how far Britain lagged behind Western Europe and the United States of America in library provision. British library borrowing was examined by the Committee in some depth. The majority of books borrowed were from circulating libraries. It has been suggested that by 1821 there were around 1,500 circulating libraries each with about seventy subscribers. But no one really knows how many tobacconists and street hawkers also hired out books at 1d a volume.

Between them the circulating libraries hired out millions of books a year.

The Committee were given details of subscription libraries and the rapidly growing religious libraries. It is estimated that between them the Society for Promoting Christian Knowledge and the Religious Tract Society established over 4,000 libraries between 1832 and 1849. These 'libraries' obviously varied in size and the stock had a religious leaning but it was an attempt to make literature available to more people.

The Committee were very interested in a type of religious library that had been introduced into East Lothian early in 1817, by one Samuel Brown. Brown's object had been to provide a library within a mile and a half of every inhabitant in the country. An ambitious project. Books in lots of fifty were placed in every village or hamlet where a librarian and suitable storing premises could be found. The books were changed periodically and the cost borne by Brown and his friends. Initially the scheme was very successful and copied in different parts of the country, but when a charge of 1d per volume was introduced a decline set in.

Private subscription libraries did not generally cater for working men, mechanics or artisans, who were often eager for self education. To meet this need, institutions sprang up throughout the nineteenth century. The Mechanics Institutes are probably the best known. In 1823 the London Mechanics Institutes, now Birkbeck College, was formed, immediately attracting some 13,000 working men as members. The movement spread rapidly. In 1851 it is estimated that there were 610 institutes in England with a total membership of 600,000. An essential feature of each institute was the library. Samuel Smiles said of the Yorkshire Mechanics Institute:
"that it was necessary to have a library to keep the institute together".

The number of books lent by the institutes is impressive. In 1849 four hundred institutes had between them three and four hundred thousand volumes, with an annual circulation of more than a million. The number of institutes grew. But these libraries were not free and not strictly public. As the Select Committee could not fail to grasp, the country had thousands of libraries, but good libraries were rare and good free public libraries were almost non-existent.

George Dawson, a non-conformist minister reported to the Committee:
"we give the people of this country an appetite to read and then supply them with nothing".

At a time when less than 8 per cent of the nation's children attended school this was hardly true, but the issue had become rather emotive. The Select Committee passed on their recommendations and, not without opposition, the Public Libraries Act, 1850 became law in August of that year. Broadly speaking the Act gave municipal boroughs with a population of 10,000 or more the option to spend a rate not exceeding one half penny in the pound on the provision of accommodation for a Public Library or Museum of Art and Science or both. It did not permit expenditure on books, as it was hoped they would be donated. Town Councils wishing to adopt the Act had to conduct a special poll of the ratepayers, a majority of two-thirds of the votes cast being necessary to secure adoption. The early years of the 1850 Act and subsequent amendments that increased the rate limit to one penny, authorised the purchase of books and newspapers, empowered the dismissal as well as appointment of staff and changed population requirements for adopting the Public Library Acts. Apart from a unifying measure in 1892, when all earlier English Public Library legislation was amalgamated into one Act, it remained the principal piece of legislation until 1919. During the period mentioned the Malacious Damages Act of 1861 made any person destroying or damaging books in any library, museum or art gallery open to the public, liable to imprisonment for six months with or without hard labour and if a male, with or without whipping. The Act has now been repealed.

The early years of the first act and subsequent amendments saw a gradual flowering of the public library movement. The City of Norwich was the first municipality to take advantage of the 1850 Act. After Norwich progress was gradual. Twenty-eight libraries were established between 1851 and 1867 and many authorities tried to open a library without gaining the required majority. Ninety-nine libraries were established in the years 1868 to 1886, and a further 224 between 1886 and the turn of the century. A pattern had been established by 1886. Dr

9

Thomas Kelly has suggested that 1887, the year of Queen Victoria's Jubilee, aroused a patriotic fervour resulting in an urge to erect statues and build libraries. Certainly this was true of Wolverhampton which had adopted the Act in 1869, but desperately needed a new Central Library. Jubilee attempts to raise money towards a new library included sponsored football matches by the staff through the streets.

But what of mobile libraries in an era of horses and railways, in a time when attempts were being made to provide libraries for all the people? Although circulating and itinerant libraries certainly made attempts to get books to the people, often regardless of the distance involved, and were certainly mobile; the first recorded instance of readers borrowing books directly from a vehicle was a horse drawn van in Warrington, where, in 1859, the Mechanics Institute inaugurated a perambulating library for the working classes. The directors of the Warrington branch of the Mechanics Institute had found difficulty in raising the circulation of the library above 3,000 volumes a year:

"and these not among the working classes to the extent which the directors desired, owing to the difficulty of getting working men to wash their faces and come to the library bar and ask for a book".

So the directors purchased, with money raised by working men of Warrington, a van, horse and books for £275; and took the books to the people. During the first year almost 12,000 books were borrowed from the perambulating library and great hopes for the future were raised.

During the second half of the nineteenth century the Mechanics Institutes were prominent in the movement of taking books to areas where libraries were not available. The Warrington perambulating library was one of the most revolutionary library advances of the nineteenth century. But in the same part of the country an equally revolutionary programme was under way. As the Mechanics Institutes became numerous they organised themselves for more efficiency into Unions. Three of these Unions, the Lancashire and Cheshire, Yorkshire and Northern Unions started a service to non-library areas modelled on the itinerating libraries introduced by Samuel Brown in East Lothian in 1817. The service operated by the

Mechanics Unions used the boxes of books system but expanded it considerably. Of the three the best known was the Yorkshire Union established in 1852. By 1891, it had an aggregate membership of 60,380 and a village library of 30,000 serving about 200 villages from a central store in Leeds. The number of books issued in 1890-1891 was almost 34,000. Another Union, that of the Lancashire and Cheshire Institutes formed in 1839, soon had a membership of 50,000, while the third Union operating a library service to villages in the area, the Northern Union, was founded in 1848. The three Unions were united in 1856 and were still flourishing at the end of the century. The Mechanics Institutes had recognised early in the day, the importance of reaching those who could not or would not use the libraries that were being established. As Thomas Greenwood wrote of the service in 1892:

"Boxes of fifty or a hundred books are sent out periodically to Mechanics Institutes and working men's clubs, and the books find their way into every part of that great country; and the weaver the ploughman, the collier and the fisherman are all reached by that association".

By the time Greenwood had arrived at such conclusions, the contrast between rural and urban provisions was obvious. Travelling bookboxes seemed the immediate answer to the library needs of the rural community, but forward-thinking librarians had already realized that a county library service was the real answer.

One reason why so few advances were made in mobile library provision during the second half of the nineteenth century was that nearly all library developments were in urban areas. With few exceptions the larger authorities did not use any form of mobile library to reach the outlying areas of their cities; they built branch libraries. Liverpool built the first branch library in 1853, Manchester built her first five years later and by 1886 almost one hundred branch libraries had been opened, of which one quarter were in Leeds. One can understand such thinking; to convert a shop or build a branch was much simpler than taking a horse and book van round the streets.

This thinking was certainly reflected in 1905 when it was advocated that no reader should be obliged to go more than three quarters of a mile to his public library and that a branch library should exist for every 25-30,000 inhabitants.

But a building programme of this nature at the turn of the

PROPOSAL FOR A TRAVELLING LIBRARY

century was rarely, if ever, possible. So delivery stations or travelling libraries were organised in several large towns to meet any inadequacies. The delivery stations were usually shops, the owner taking in requests for books from readers, the list sent to the Central Library, and, it was hoped, the books were brought on the next visit of the travelling library. The system obviously had limitations.

James Duff Brown, the first Borough Librarian of Islington, regarded the delivery station as nothing more than a stop-gap until a travelling library could be introduced. Brown, from whose pen flowed such sound advice to librarians as:
"If you cannot classify a book don't buy it "
"A book in the hand is worth two at the binders "
had preferred the use of a travelling library as a means of reaching outlying districts. His interpretation of a travelling library was boxes of books deposited at a centre and periodically changed. In an article, "The Village Library Problem", that appeared in 1894 Brown foresaw the time when books could be delivered door to door by means of travelling libraries on wheels. What Brown was actually advocating was a mobile

James Duff Brown

Leen Side Reading room (closed 1889): Nottingham Public Libraries

library in the now accepted sense of the term. Brown was a far-sighted thinker in terms of library management. He introduced and pleaded for open access in public libraries. Pointing out the necessity of mobile libraries was just another example of Brown's thinking.

Brown was not alone in this idea; an anonymous letter to the Editor of *Books Queries* in November 1895 suggested: "where a branch library is not available the best alternative would be to send out each day in different directions two or three large vans or libraries on wheels, containing in each about 1,000 books arranged on shelves . . . Of course the assistant in charge would require some knowledge of horses and driving."

Despite these revolutionary ideas, book boxes, delivery stations and travelling libraries were still the chief way of getting books to readers without ready access to a branch library. Delivery stations were never meant to be permanent and at the 1903 Library Association Conference there was opposition to delivery stations on the grounds that in local government temporary often becomes permanent.

Delivery stations, which did deserve some opposition, played an essential part in branch and mobile library develop-

14

ment. The first delivery station was opened in Nottingham as early as 1879 and twenty years later Nottingham Public Libraries had three delivery stations in operation. They were basically reading rooms and were a supplement, never a replacement, for branch libraries. Travelling libraries were used in conjunction with the growth of delivery stations. Bournemouth used them between 1898 and 1899 while in 1904 Warrington Town Council adopted a scheme to establish shops in outlying parts of the town as delivery stations for books from the Central Library. In Warrington the cost per year for delivery horse and cart was £20 per station.

Although Lancashire County Library eventually operated more travelling libraries than any other authority, Bradford certainly was the largest municipal user. Bradford Public Libraries introduced the first travelling library in October, 1902. Each delivery station or centre was provided with a collection of about 320 volumes of carefully selected books, which after remaining one year were passed on to the next locality. Thus each centre was served with an entirely fresh stock once a year. Originally there were six delivery stations, but by 1903, owing to the excessive use made of them, it became necessary to open them two evenings, which by 1906 supplied the needs of about 750 readers. The exchanges were carried out by horse and cart and made use of four open tins to hold the books. Problems with the tins were nothing compared with the horses. Mr R. Garnett, recently retired from Bradford Public Libraries, recalls being sent to a centre to replace an injured porter. As the injured man was carried away his parting words to Mr Garnett were:

"Remember to put the nose bag on the horse at one o'clock."

With no previous experience of driving a horse and cart Ronnie Garnett was left with the problem of geting the horse and cart back to the Central Library and found it something of a trial!

Hired motor vans replaced horses as a means of serving the Bradford delivery stations from 1934.

By the end of the nineteenth century travelling libraries as an attempt to make books more available were increasingly important. In 1895 a circulating library for working girls was established in London and travelling libraries were becoming commonplace overseas.

In the United States the Missouri State Federation of Women's Clubs reported fifteen travelling libraries, each library capable of containing fifty volumes which could be retained for a 4 to 6 month period for a two and a half dollars fee.

It was in the United States, Hagerstown, Washington County, Maryland, that the first twentieth century mobile library was established in 1907. Drawn by two horses and carrying a stock of 300 books the book waggon was very popular. As the librarian Miss Mary Titcomb pointed out:
"To drive a book waggon is an all round job but one that brings its own rewards in the respect and affection won..."

By 1914 many states in the United States already had a system of travelling libraries as a means of reaching the 55 per cent of the population who did not live in urban areas. New York State had the most extensive and flourishing system of travelling libraries. The system was not without its critics:
"The few people reached compared with the great rural population of the state of New York, wherein the travelling library under the direction of the State Library Commission

1907 Maryland mobile library

seems to be more widely used than in any other state of the Union, indicates the futility of trying by means of a travelling library system operated from the capitol of the state, to supply farm homes with library privileges."
(S.B. and E.I. Antrim. *The County Library*. American Library Association, 1914.)

But as British libraries came to grips with the twentieth century an event took place that was to lay the foundations for modern mobile library provision. This was the purchase in 1904 by Glasgow Public Libraries of a library delivery vehicle.

Glasgow Public Libraries had made phenomenal progress, not adopting the Public Libraries Act until 1899, after the third attempt, but fifteen years later having a bookstock of 468,000, easily the largest of any public library system in the country. They were helped by benefactors who donated to the city for library development £200,000 over a thirty year period. Andrew Carnegie in 1901 offered £100,000 for branch library development. The delivery vehicle was used to carry one thousand books a week round the branch libraries. Cost in 1905, £1 a week. Glasgow was to prove that isolated branch libraries reading rooms and readers could be served far more effectively by motor vehicle than by horse and cart. This set something of a precedent that other authorities were to follow.

By the beginning of the twentieth century literature had already appeared on the subject of mobile libraries: F. A. Hutchins, *Travelling Libraries,* published in 1902 by the American Library Association.

2. Municipalities: The Forerunners

It is no accident that the municipal library authorities were the forerunners and innovators in mobile library development. Legislation to allow the formation of a County Library Service was not passed until 1919, and during the early years of county libraries opinions on the value of mobile libraries were sharply divided.

The First World War had increased motor vehicle production for the war effort and some of these surplus vehicles were acquired by library authorities. The days of the horse-drawn delivery vehicles and travelling libraries were not over but were certainly numbered. Branch library building and mobile library provision was the immediate answer to an expanding urban population in the decade following the end of the First World War. The building of branch libraries did not get under way until the mid twenties and became more important as the population spread from the old town centres to the suburban housing estates. As the number of branch libraries increased and readers requested a changing stock, various methods were favoured by librarians for geting books to the branches. During the Library Association Conference at Manchester in 1921, a Mr Houghton, Librarian of Worksop, advocated the use of a extending and completing such provision throughout England and Wales."

In 1927 the Kenyon Report noted that 96.3 per cent of the population of England and Wales were within the area of library authorities. Despite this impressive statistic, in rural areas half the population were without a library service. Kenyon felt the travelling library was the best way to provide a rural library service. However, the Kenyon definition of a travelling library was a small collection of books, perhaps 30 to 50 volumes, which were available for loan as a unit to isolated groups of readers and changed as requested.

But Manchester Public Libraries were about to alter for ever the definition of a travelling library. Manchester had an effective branch library system before the First World War and in fact did not build any branch libraries between the wars. But the new housing estates grew, demanding a library service. Yet money did not exist to build branch libraries. Stanley Jast, the City Librarian of Manchester, had noted that a delivery vehicle with books could go anywhere in the city, including the new estates remote from existing branch libraries. Jast was aware of

The first municipal mobile library introduced by Manchester Public Libraries in July 1931

L. Stanley Jast,
Librarian of Peterborough 1892–98,
Croydon 1898–1915, Manchester 1920–31.

developments overseas, having visited libraries in the United States where mobile libraries were in extensive use. From Jast came Manchester's "bibliobus", the first mobile library to become a regular and recognised feature of any library authority in the United Kingdom. The vehicle, a discarded but still workable 1917 single-decker bus acquired from the city transport department, took to the streets in 1931. The bibliobus provided open access for a maximum of 20 readers to select from a stock of 1300 volumes on sloped shelves. It was described by Jast as a "small branch library on wheels which returns at night for supplies". Providing a floor area of approximately 84 sq.ft with ample accommodation for about twenty readers at one time and carrying a stock that was replenished each day from a total stock of about 6,000, the travelling library was an immediate success. "Gratifying" is how the City Librarian described the increase in monthly issue figures from 834 in July to 10,908 the following March. He did

A chance meeting between the City Librarian of Manchester and the Chairman of Erith Library Committee solved Erith's lack of branch libraries: the introduction of a mobile library. At a cost of £685, Erith's mobile library took to the streets in April 1933 and was successful from the first trip

not add that the bibliobus accidently chose a piece of soft ground on its first day out and had to be unceremoniously towed back onto firm ground!

The type of problems experienced by Manchester: rapid housing estate development of the thirties without the money to build branch libraries, were common all over the country. By the mid-thirties the Carnegie United Kingdom Trust were assisting the new social services rather than contributing to the public library. The Trustees' report for 1936 was the first since the foundation in which library policy played a relatively small part. Without Carnegie or funds from central government it appeared that library development to non-library areas would be very gradual.

Erith in Kent had a large housing development on the west of the town without library provision. Four branch libraries were needed to provide an adequate service and this was out of the question. Then a chance meeting between Jast of Manchester and the Chairman of Erith Library Committee solved the problem. The Chairman visited Manchester, was impressed with the travelling library and approval was given for a similar venture in Erith. Not without opposition, a converted van of pantechnicon shape on a two-ton Fordson chassis took to the streets of Erith in 1933. Costing £685 and holding up to 2,000 books it was successful from its first trip. In the first year, 1,658 new borrowers were registered and almost 59,000 books issued. Annual running costs worked out at £105. Comments about mobile libraries began appearing in the professional press. Mr James Ormerod of Derby suggested in 1932 that a tram or trolleybus once stripped of its seats might be used as a travelling library in the thinly-populated and distant parts of our towns and cities.

The third of the five pre-war mobile libraries introduced by municipal authorities took to the streets of Burnley in 1936. An articulated delivery van previously used for the distribution of school meals, the vehicle was pressed into service by Burnley Public Libraries. Operating until 1938, the vehicle was never intended to be anything other than a stop-gap until the building of static service points.

As the Burnley mobile was withdrawn from service, Manchester Public Libraries introduced a second vehicle to replace the first. Again almost embarrassingly successful, the travelling library had a daily average issue of 423 and by the end of the year this had increased to 848. The second vehicle was operational until 1940 when it was withdrawn owing to war problems and not re-introduced until 1948. The only other municipal authority to introduce a mobile library before the outbreak of World War 2 was Hastings. Introduced from February 1938, the library held slightly more than 2,000 books on a three-ton, 6-wheel chassis and was powered by a Ford 30hp engine. As the war placed more of a strain on Hastings Libraries the mobile was offered to any authority that could make use of it.

The London Borough of St Pancras's hopes for library expansion were halted by the war. Efforts were being made to continue the service but this was proving difficult until the

*London's first mobile library, serving the readers of St. Pancras. (Above)
1941. (Below) 1945*

Borough Librarian heard about the Hastings mobile. Claimed to be London's first mobile library, the vehicle caught the imagination of press and public alike. It is hardly surprising St Pancras welcomed the mobile with a library publicity previously unknown in that part of London. Local papers, handbills, circulars, films and a specially designed poster bearing the slogan "A Library to Your Door" were displayed all over the Borough. At the opening ceremony the Mayor gave his blessing to this "library of wheels" saying "People without books are like houses without windows".

The mobile was intended solely as a war time measure, as an aid to those who could not reach a branch library because of the disruption of war. Holding two-thirds non-fiction stock and a good choice of children's books, the mobile was very successful, with 2,000 new readers joining in the first month. When the service was terminated in 1946 the public let the Borough Librarian know in no uncertain terms that it was missed.

The war effort obviously put a halt to any real development in mobile library provision though in 1942 the Emergency Committee of the Library Association placed on record the hope that the Petroleum Department would not limit the supply for essential journeys of library vehicles, including mobile libraries. The resolution may have had some effect because in the same year West Ham Libraries introduced a converted van into service as a mobile library. The vehicle was used to serve the new housing estates in the same pattern as Manchester and Erith.

Despite a lack of petrol and staff every effort was made to keep books and libraries mobile during the war years. The wartime conditions such as reduction in transport facilities and hours of waiting all increased the reading habit. Public libraries recorded increased use and tried to cope with often double and treble issue figures. But just where travelling libraries could have been most use, visiting military and evacuee camps, the vehicles, staff or petrol were not available.

Although travelling libraries were used to serve Civil Defence workers and Barrage Balloon personnel, travelling libraries in the form of book boxes came back to the fore with air-raid shelter libraries introduced to at least fourteen London districts. Boxes of books travelled around the shelters to help pass away the hours for those gathered in them. One of the most ambitious shelter libraries was in a tube station at Bethnal Green; with a changing book stock of 4,000 volumes it was open from 5.30 to 8.00pm, Monday to Saturday, and served a population of 6,000 shelterers.

Throughout the world mobile libraries continued to provide service during the war years. The travelling library introduced by the Leningrad Professional Union of Metal Workers served 8,000 children throughout the war years, including the siege of Leningrad. It was half-way through the war years that the most devastating and perhaps most influential of all library reports was produced. The McColvin Report or *The public library system of Great Britain: a report on its present condition with proposals for a post war re-organisation* was published by the Library Association in 1942. McColvin described the basic methods adopted by county libraries for providing a library service to isolated areas. Additional facilities to these basic methods included van delivery to individuals or families. The travelling library:
"a van in which a stock is displayed and available for selection" was obviously going to be the method to serve small communities and individual readers in the future. Travelling libraries were included in McColvin's proposals for the future. But they were to take second place to library centres.

Advances in mobile libraries were not always what you would expect. In Baltimore, a horse and cart with books was re-introduced in 1943, as a mobile library to help solve juvenile delinquency problems because the children preferred the horse to the motor vehicle.

3. Mobile Libraries and the New County Libraries

The modern county library service gained its roots on the 3rd October 1913, the date when the Carnegie United Kingdom Trust was formed.

Andrew Carnegie left his native Dunfermline at the age of twelve to emigrate to America, where he immediately started work. He retired fifty-four years later, master of the largest iron and steel corporation in the world. His fortune was worth hundreds of millions of dollars and he proposed to give much of it away to good causes. As he had access to the private library of a retired manufacturer early in his career Carnegie realised the value of books in terms of education and recreational pleasure. Among the good causes Carnegie particularly favoured were church organs and public libraries. Carnegie's benefactors started in a small way. In 1879 he offered £8,000 to his native Dunfermline to build a public library. Grants went to other Scottish towns and cities. In 1897 an executive officer was appointed to handle applications for grants and assistance. By 1919 there were nearly three thousand Carnegie Public Libraries in different parts of the world. Wishing to continue this benevolence Carnegie placed at the disposal of the Carnegie United Kingdom Trust the annual interest produced on an investment of ten million dollars. This interest in 1919 alone was worth in excess of £100,000 per year. Despite such odd donations as Carnegie giving £10,000 so that a library could be built for an authority that only had £1 to spend on books, the debt the public library movement owes to this investment is beyond measure.

The Executive Committee of the Carnegie United Kingdom Trust was, like the Parliamentary Select Committee of 1849, wise enough to realise that before it could determine library policy it must have as complete a picture as possible of existing library provision. From this desire for the complete library picture came the Adams Report on the Library Provision and Policy of the Carnegie United Kingdom Trustees, prepared by

Wiltshire County Library Headquarters, 1923. The Headquarters were purchased from the Canadian Army at the end of the first World War for £100. The photograph shows the County Librarian, Mr. C. Hamilton, and two of his staff, together with some of the lead-lined book boxes that were then transported by rail to the various village centres. The first van delivery scheme was introduced to Wiltshire in 1928 but the lead-lined boxes remained in use until the sixties.

Professor W.G.S. Adams of Oxford University in 1914 and published a year later. In many ways the report laid the foundations for county library provision for the next few decades. It pointed out that library development had taken place in areas of concentrated population and now was the time to correct the imbalance:

"to prepare the way for the gradual but certain extension of a national rural library scheme of rate-supported libraries"

It further stated that such developments should take place in association with educational institutes in rural areas and in close association with, if not under the control of, the county education committee. Emphasis was continually placed on the

27

importance of a changing supply of books, based on a central distributing point administered by:

"A new corps of librarians, in the form of county library superintendents will be required if the movement is to be progressively developed".

A changing supply of books was not new; the itinerating libraries of the previous century and the Mechanics Institutes had carried out much of what the report recommended. The report advocated that experimental schemes, financed by the Trustees, should be attempted in different parts of the United Kingdom. The C.U.K.T. as the organisation came to be known, were as good as their word, taking over and financing such schemes as the Coats Libraries of the Highlands and Islands of Scotland. These libraries, initiated by Sir Peter Coates of Paisley numbered 315 in all. Supplied from a central repository at Dunfermline books were changed quarterly, and over 100,000 books were issued in the first five years of the scheme, proving beyond doubt that a demand existed even in the most remote area for a comprehensive library service. During the experiment an account exists of a shepherd a long way from any library being supplied with a book tied to the back of his dog. A mobile library of sorts, even with a limited stock, but certainly not the first!

Other schemes assisted by the C.U.K.T. included a grant of £1,000 given in 1905 towards the formation of a system of circulating libraries in Herefordshire. The system devised by Dr Percival, Bishop of Hereford, consisted of boxes of books distributed to villages in his diocese at a cost of £1 per year per village. A similar system established by Sir Henry Peto for the county of Dorset in 1907 also received help. Under the Peto system boxes of books were distributed three times a year to schools and village institutes for an annual charge of £1 per year, one quarter of the charge being met by the local education authority.

The first county, as opposed to privately sponsored schemes, to take advantage of the offer of experimental schemes financed by the C.U.K.T. was Staffordshire. The C.U.K.T. offered Staffordshire £5,000 to be spent over 5 years on a central repository, a stock of books, travelling boxes, administration and carriage; asking only that:

28

There is little doubt that the C.U.K.T. helped lay the foundations of the county library service. The Public Libraries Act 1919 Sect. 1 (1) stated:

". . . The Council of any county in England or Wales shall have power by resolution specifying the area to which the resolution extends to adopt the Public Libraries Acts for the whole or any part of their county, exclusive of any part of the county which is an existing library area . . . "

Under Section 5 of the Education (Scotland) Act, 1918, it became possible to establish a county library service in Scotland. Similar legislation was passed for Northern Ireland in 1924.

The county libraries were legally born, and when the first county librarians needed guidance about services to isolated areas, the various experimental schemes sponsored and financed by the C.U.K.T. had been established to do just that. The Adams Report had emphasised the need for library provision in rural areas and the only successful way of achieving this was through village centre collections which were period-ically changed. With the problem of having to establish a library headquarters that might be converted stables, an inn or

The first county book delivery van: Perthshire County Library 1921

Middlesex County book delivery van, 1926. Note the shelving

a former prison with initial financial assistance often as low as 1/18d rate, village centres were the only realistic way of establishing a service of sorts. Many derelict and declining subscription librries were taken over as village centres. However, the majority of centres, again as the Adams Report recommended, were in schools with a school teacher acting as volunteer librarian. E.J. Carnell of Lancashire County Library summed up the Adams Report as presenting three ideas: the county council as a library authority, the circulating system based on a central collection and the voluntary helper. Other definitions of the early days of county libraries have included: "the era of the village centre" or "the box of books era".

By 1925 with the exception of Westmorland, Lincolnshire-Holland, Rutland, Isles of Scilly, Carmarthen and Argyllshire, all county councils in England, Wales and Scotland had provided a library service of sorts. All the new library authorities had a similar problem: a way of getting books to readers in rural communities.

The village centre was obviously the only feasible place to house the books but geting the books to the centre was a feat in itself. The books were generally transported in boxes and great importance was attached to these boxes. The Adams Report even mentioned the screws on the boxes used in Dorset, Westmorland and Yorkshire. The geographical limitations of many counties made the boxes the life blood of the library service. The boxes varied in size, but all appeared to be back-breaking when empty, let alone when filled with books! Organized by C.U.K.T. the 1920 Rural Library Conference on "Transport Problems" show the costs against different methods of transporting boxes:

Gloucestershire:	Rail/Carrier/Double Journey	4s. 1d	
	Hired Van	5s. 0d	
	Authority Van	3s. 3d	
		per box	
Nottinghamshire:	Hire Van	5s. 4½d	
		per box	
Warwickshire:	Hired Motor Transport	2s. 6d	flat rate
		per box	
Middlesex:	Hired Motor Transport	5d	per book
		on a double journey	

A village library exchange carried out by Kent mobile library, 1928

Kent County Library exhibition vehicle

Great disparity existed in the reports involving costs varying between 11s and 1s 8d per box. But it soon became obvious that as long as transport was needed to circulate the stock of the village centres, the cheapest way of doing this was by authority-owned vehicles. Realizing this, Perthshire became the first county to acquire a book delivery van in 1920, a light Ford van with shelves to hold eight to nine hundred books, and which went into service early in 1921. Kent followed suit in 1924, purchasing in 1924, a 30 cwt Vulcan covered lorry with shelves to hold two thousand books. Costing £625 with conversions, the lorry was initially more expensive than train or carrier, but as it was making six to eight calls a day, it was offering a much better service. The County Librarian was obviously pleased with it:

"The van has covered 14,000 miles this year with only one small delay. In one year 826 visits were paid to centres and 105,005 books were issued from the van".

By 1925 Lindsey, Norfolk, Northumberland, Oxfordshire and the East Riding of Yorkshire were also operating vans. The Northumberland vehicle covered 6,953 miles in 1926, four to eight centres visited daily. The librarian always accompanied the van and the cost (including depreciation) was 5.53d per mile. Surrey's van was described as "fast, reliable and comfortable". The vehicle, a Morris 25 cwt, cost £315.

In 1926 the counties appeared to be divided between owning or hiring a van, but the railways were still a popular way to transport books, though Breconshire and Bedfordshire still recommended the bus as a mode of transporting books. Despite these changes, in 1928 over half the counties still used the railways as the chief means of getting books to centres.

Gloucestershire County Library mobile: Berkeley Vale 1958

Kent County exhibition library. Note the mascot!

Miss A. S. Cooke, County Librarian of Gloucester, 1918-21, and of Kent, 1921-43, innovator of mobile libraries

Perthshire and Kent, with the introduction of motorized book deliveries, had created important landmarks.

During the early years of village centres, the collections were treated as single units and moved as a unit within a chain system. Before the introduction of motor transport often the complete collection of books had to be returned to head-quarters and checked off before being passed on to the next centre. Should the collection not be complete, correspond-ence would build up between H.Q. and the centre, and until the problems were sorted out the centre would often be without books for several weeks. With motor transport, books could be delivered and the old collection checked off at the same time. The stock would be changed three or four times a year, creating a far better choice for readers. But the van system did have its faults: readers were still rarely allowed to borrow straight from the van. The idea was to change the centre collection; the visits were short and often books were changed without the librarian/volunteer being present. An ideal transport system must provide speed, flexibility, publicity, economy and be a direct link between library H.Q. and reader. During the years leading up to the last war small light vans seemed to answer most of these requirements.

By 1927 Kent had added a second delivery van, a two ton Thornycroft capable of holding 2,500 books. The use of pneumatic tyres had considerably reduced the fatigue inci-dental to long busy days on the road. As the County Librarian stated:

"The distribution of books has been done for three years now by motor van instead of by boxes, and it becomes increasingly evident that this method is the better".

Using the additional vehicle it became possible to visit all Kent's centres three times a year. That progress was being made became obvious in 1926 at the Library Association Conference when it was recommended that vehicles should be fitted with headlamps. By 1928 various opinions on the types of transport still reigned. Six counties still used steamships to help with book circulation but this did mean that 64 out of 80 Scottish lighthouses were regularly served. In the 1928/9 C.U.K.T. Report it appeared that the majority of county librarians agreed that some form of motor transport was preferable to rail or carrier. But one controversy still raged: the superiority of the exhibition vehicle over the delivery van. The exhibition vehicle, being fitted with shelving, allowed the local librarian, teacher or reader to select books direct from the vehicle for the centre or branch library. Exhibition vans were usually built on a 20 cwt or 30 cwt chassis and had shelf accommodation for between 1000-2000 volumes. This was the type of vehicle used by among others, Perthshire, Kent, Norfolk, Northumberland and the East Riding of Yorkshire.

Originally the shelves were arranged in alcoves with exterior access but in 1925 Lindsey County introduced an interior access, which held fewer books but gave protection from the easterly elements. Lindsey were far-sighted to employ a chauffeur to drive the vehicle, so the librarian, who was given a folding table and portable typewriter, could deal with administration en route. As the C.U.K.T. Report for 1926/7 states: "... there is something heroic in the picture of a librarian typing his letters and memoranda in a van doing thirty to forty miles an hour even on the relatively level roads of Lincolnshire".

The exhibition van with interior access was a mobile library in all but name in 1925. That the exhibition vehicle secured excellent publicity could not be doubted. Norfolk County Library introduced an exhibition vehicle in 1926 and within a year had doubled the number of borrowers and issues for the area. The county librarian reported:
"We have found the van system of transport most satisfactory. The van is divided into three compartments, fiction, non-fiction and juvenile fiction — and a certain proportion is chosen from each section".

The County Librarian of Northamptonshire agreed:
"Experience shows that the time will come when we shall need to improve the method of circulation between headquarters and the branches. At present we employ a motor lorry about once a fortnight for the conveyance of books; ... The ideal method is the fitted book van.."

The other type of delivery to centres and branches was favoured by among others, Surrey, West Sussex, Wiltshire and Middlesex: the delivery van. Initially simply a van used to carry book-boxes, Middlesex in 1927 added the more sensible method of book trays fitting into racks in the van. The controversy over book vans against exhibition vehicles reigned until the beginning of the last war. The 1928/9 Report of the C.U.K.T. also shows that despite advances in taking books direct to readers, local centres still remained the back-bone of the county library movement. Some authorities realized that their library provision was not complete simply because boxes of books were sent to centres every three months; but as 60 per cent of centres in England, 48 per cent in Wales, 54 per cent in Scotland and 63 per cent in Ireland received fewer than 100 books per quarter, provision was still inadequate. Larger centres were being established and smaller ones amalgamated, but already it was becoming obvious that mobile libraries offering a service direct to readers were the answer to the library needs of scattered communities.

In 1935 Kent County Library, a forerunner in many library developments, introduced the first County Mobile Library offering a service as we know mobile libraries today. Miss A.S. Cooke, the County Librarian of Kent, understood the limitations of mobile libraries, indeed on one occasion referred to that arm of the library service as "spoon-feeding" the readers.

But early in 1935 a travelling library van began visiting the urban district of Chislehurst and Sidcup in Kent. The vehicle, which had been formerly used for the general distribution of books throughout the whole county, had been re-fitted to enable books to be issued to the borrowers by an assistant working from inside the van. It visited four districts on the outskirts of the area, and remained on site for a few hours on two or three days a week. This revolutionary move in county library thinking was not widely reported in the professional press as had been the mobile library development in Manchester and Erith. Miss Cooke described the development in two sentences in a short article that appeared in the LAR in 1937.

The year Kent introduced its first mobile library, 1935, saw the publication by the Library Association of a *County Libraries Manual* that had a section dealing with exhibition vans but still advocated that the village centre was the only means of providing a rural library service.

However, at the A.G.M. of the County Libraries section of the Library Association in 1938, an apparently new development of a service taking books direct to readers was discussed. A mobile library service of sorts had already been introduced to Warrington, Manchester, Lincolnshire, Burnley and Kent.

Early in 1938, James Brindle, area Librarian for Ulverston with Lancashire County Library had been using an exhibition vehicle to serve thirty nine centres in schools and village institutes. He also changed the books at an additional one hundred plus stops offering a service to families in remote areas. Brindle's idea was to supply a service direct to one hundred and nineteen families each month using the exhibition vehicle. Books were issued on a family basis without limit to number or character. The van had an issue desk and was in every sense a mobile library. The service was immediately successful and as a result of this development it became possible to close fifteen of the smaller centres.

An important development as it undoubtably was, not every County Librarian thought this was the answer to rural library provision. Miss Cooke, who had introduced the first county mobile library three years previously, had been critical of such a service. Miss E.J. Carnell in her book *County Libraries*, published in 1938, while admitting that a scattered population can be served by van added:
". . . the van could not achieve the half of the work which is now being done by keen and enthusiastic local librarians."
Twenty-four years after the Adams Report the place of the volunteer was not forgotten.

So on the eve of the Second World War total library issues were nearly 250 millions. An increase of 20 per cent in only four years and the number of county library readers had increased by 87 per cent between 1932-9, Lancashire, Lincolnshire and Kent were the only counties operating a mobile library service. But the next decade was to change that picture forever.

4. Rapid Developments

During the late 1940's, as the United Kingdom recovered from the last war, important changes were taking place in the attitude towards readers in small and often isolated communities. Although in 1946 the combined county libraries operated only six mobile libraries between them, the position was changing rapidly. In 1949 B. Oliph Smith, the County Librarian of the West Riding of Yorkshire, had stated:

". . . the countryman is entitled to just as good a service as the urban dweller, and the only hope of giving it to him lies in considerable development of the use of mobile libraries".

Smith, in many ways the father of modern mobile library services, practised what he preached. The West Riding of Yorkshire, a region about ninety miles north to south, sixty miles east to west, including much industrialisation, but with large areas that were sparsely populated and often mountainous, was a challenge to any librarian. Problems of basic administration were staggering. A journey from HQ to the most distant branch involved a round trip of 170 miles. In August 1949 there were 84 branch libraries, but, for communities below 1,000 population level, the only library provision was the experimental travelling library service.

When County Librarian of Herefordshire, Smith had been critical of the limited mobile service operated by Lancashire County Library to North Lonsdale, introduced in 1938. He considered monthly visits insufficient yet the introduction of even such an insufficient service to Herefordshire would be impossibly expensive.

But in the West Riding of Yorkshire Smith had the opportunity to introduce a travelling library service. The mobile library was initially ordered and organised by Miss E. F. Wragg, the Acting County Librarian, in 1945. The County Library Committee purchased an ex-ARP ambulance for use in the Bowland district of the county as a travelling library van. The vehicle, a 12 hp Renault, held 300 books and, being cream with

B. Oliph Smith, the father of mobile libraries, with John Masefield opening a branch library in Herefordshire, 1938

scarlet lettering, the van, when on the high fell tracks, could be seen for miles. It was called Minerva after the goddess of wisdom and it marked the beginning of an era. "Minnie", as the staff called her, travelled 225 miles of road on four routes, each to be covered once a fortnight. In the more remote areas the staff also acted as unofficial postmen and carriers of news. No children's books were carried and A.G. Street was the most popular author. Minnie's real test came in the winter of 1947 when the staff went out armed with chains, rope, a spade, bricks, flasks of tea and a hot water bottle. After her first full year some interesting statistics were produced. Of the population served by Minnie, only 37 per cent lived in villages, the remainder being scattered over the rest of the area served. Non-fiction accounted for more than 25 per cent of the issue

40

while more books were borrowed in the fertile areas than in the poor fell lands. Minnie set something of a precedent. The mobile library, at comparatively little cost, made a comprehensive library service available to all.

Changes came slowly in the immediate post-war years. This was understandable; the priority was to re-house and to re-employ. Many authorities, realizing the advantages of mobile libraries, wanted to introduce them. Owing to lack of materials the authorities who introduced mobile libraries had to convert almost anything on wheels into a mobile library or argue very convincingly for a custom-built vehicle!

Kingston-on-Thames was one authority that needed a mobile library. Money was not available for a custom-built vehicle, and so in 1946 a converted mobile kitchen trailer was put into service. Leigh Public Libraries introduced a converted 1931 Leyland bus into service as a mobile library in 1947. Much interest was shown in the vehicle when it was exhibited at a meeting of the North Western Branch of the Library Association held at Blackpool in 1947. The vehicle captured the imagination of all present. 1947 also saw the introduction of mobile libraries to, among others, Enfield, Hendon, Thurrock, Hornsey and Monmouthshire. New services were not always given the instant blessing of the elected representatives. During 1947 a mobile library scheme for Dumfriesshire approved by the Library Committee failed by one vote to get Council approval. Some of the comments on the proposed service reflected contemporary attitudes:

"This is utter nonsense and a lot of rot, I am against it. The country people have quite enough to do without this. When are they going to do their work?"

The post-war years were undoubtedly the years of the adaptable librarian. Those who wanted mobile libraries aimed to convert any type of vehicle to provide a service. Mr A.C. Hedges, Borough Librarian of Yarmouth, was a good example of the "adaptable". He purchased from the Yarmouth Transport Department a pre-war double-decker bus for £5. The seats were removed and sold to the Yarmouth racecourse, the additional income being used towards the conversion costs of the vehicle.

The origins of a library service to scattered communities in

Herefordshire were created in 1897 when Dr John Percival sent out small boxes of books to remote country hamlets for the "edification and enlightenment" of the inhabitants of the Diocese of the Bishop of Hereford. This was a large area, covering Herefordshire, parts of Wales and about a third of Shropshire. Andrew Carnegie helped the venture with a grant of £1500 in 1906. The service prospered and in 1926 was taken over by the newly formed Herefordshire Library Service. The problem of providing an adequate library service to these areas was solved with the introduction of a travelling library in 1947. The vehicle, a three-ton Austin ARP, was chosen because it was immediately available and was an ideal for the terrain to be covered. Converted by the library staff for £12, the vehicle held 1400 books. It operated on a six-week cycle serving 9,000 people living in approximately 250 sq. miles.

By the late forties mobile libraries were becoming established, though in 1948, 19,000 library centres were still the county library service. The large number of village centres represented a phenomenally large amount of stock lying idle for most of the time. Fifty village centres usually represented at least 10,000 books not fully utilised owing to the inadequate opening hours of most of the village centres. A mobile library could offer a constantly changing stock of approaching one thousand books. The West Riding of Yorkshire County Library had demonstrated that mobile libraries could revolutionize the reading habits of the public they served. Once the service was established the number of books borrowed was four times that of the village centres. Realising this the West Riding mobile library programme envisaged a fleet of 24 vehicles purchased over a ten year period. By May 1950 orders for 13 mobile libraries had been placed. These included nine small travelling libraries designed to serve communities of fewer than 500 people. These vehicles on an ex-forces Bedford MW chassis, completely reconditioned, were ideal for the considerable mileage on farm tracks. They were chosen for quick delivery. All carried a tow-rope and 1,000 books and cost £850 each. The West Riding had advanced ideas on both mobile library provision and design. The service to new residential areas within the county often meant the vehicle could not return to base every evening, so the staff would spend the evenings away from home. To accommodate this, the vehicles had wardrobe space, plus a small staff room with toilet and kitchen.

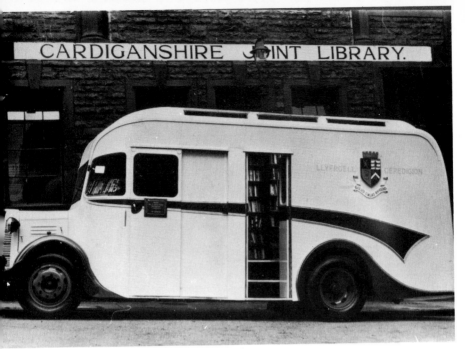

Cardiganshire Joint Library, September 1949

Manchester Public Libraries, September 1949

Leigh travelling library introduced April 1947

Herefordshire County mobile library, spring 1948

The importance of mobile libraries was clearly recognized by the Library Association with the publication in 1949 of Technical Pamphlet No 1. This dealt with mobile libraries and offered some constructive advice. Lionel McColvin was writing at the same time:

"Nothing associated with librarianship has ever caught the public imagination like the travelling library, the library on wheels, the bibliobus, an apparent practicability about the idea that to many the travelling library has become the answer to every prayer, the solution to every problem."

By the end of 1949 mobile libraries were making a significant contribution to annual reports and happenings within library authorities. Both Kesteven and Gloucestershire pointed out that mobile libraries are probably the only answer to deficiencies in small village centres. Somerset was to introduce a travelling library as an experiment. Both Staffordshire and Warwickshire had introduced two mobiles with great success. Derbyshire introduced a second vehicle based on Belper. Durham reported great success with its Murton mobile library and announced long term plans to abolish all village centres. Nottinghamshire introduced two more mobile libraries based on Ollerton and Southwell. Carmarthen planned to operate mobile libraries to all villages with a population below 700. Cardiganshire was very pleased with the first mobile, introduced in 1948 at a cost of £1,500, a gift from a grateful reader!

The first Scottish rural mobile library was introduced in the spring of 1949 and became a reality after ten years of planning by Mrs M.G. Brown, County Librarian of the Stewartry of Kirkcudbright. A 10 cwt Ford van (ex-school meals) was pressed into service. Borrowed from the education department, the van was equipped with lights and carried 600 books. Mrs Brown reported:

"Six hundred may seem an absurdly small number but to country readers too long restricted to a box of books at the local school, such a selection was riches indeed."

Twenty villages were visited fortnightly by the vehicle and 23,210 books were issued during its first year. By the following July a new vehicle based on a five-ton Austin chassis and holding 2,000 books was in service. The van was returned to education but it more than served its purpose.

Tottenham Public Library daily delivery van service, 1950

A travelling library also used for display purposes, 1950. Cost £950, it held 1,550 books

Converted from a 1932 Corporation bus and put into service in 1948, by Preston Borough Libraries, this vehicle operated until 1966.

Bedfordshire County Library, September 1949

Also in 1949, the Isle of Wight County Library introduced the first of three mobile libraries. The first vehicle opened up all parts of the Island to a vastly improved library service.

The early 'fifties continued the tradition of introducing mobile libraries gradually, converting when an authority could not afford custom-built vehicles, and finding ways round the new legislation that was affecting motor transport of all types.

To give one example of the ways in which this could be carried out, Castleford Public Libraries found a way of avoiding the annual road fund tax of £85. The mobile library they introduced was a 1932 Leyland Tiger single-decker bus converted into a trailer holding 2,500 books. It served six localities until static libraries were built. An electric kettle and fire provided for the staff made conditions easier, while exterior colouring of cherry red with "bookmobile" in red must have caught the eye of many a hesitant reader. Being a trailer it did not pay the tax.

A practice established in Manchester and Erith in the early 1930's of using mobile libraries as temporary library provision for new housing areas was re-established in the late forties. By 1949 at least 14 authorities were known to be using such vehicles, usually converted buses, visiting sites once a week. They were poor substitutes for a branch library but did provide invaluable information about where a branch library should be built.

The value of mobile libraries reached the academic world when in 1951 C.P. Hirsch of the Agricultural Economic Research Institute at Oxford University suggested that mobile libraries were the answer to rural library provision.

By 1950 many articles had appeared in the professional press on all aspects of mobile librarianship while the name for a library on wheels still remained unsettled. The local press in certain counties favoured the term "library coach".

Conversions were still the normal way to provide a mobile library in many authorities. Solihull Public Libraries found the ideal vehicle for the troublesome reader, a mobile library converted from a two-ton Austin prison van! But even with conversion problems the number of mobile libraries was growing from six in 1946 to 59 in 1951.

Some ideas to do with mobile libraries were completely new.

Buckinghamshire County Library vehicle, 1948

Hertfordshire County Library vehicle, 1948

An example of some of the rough tracks for a Durham mobile library in the late forties

Shropshire County mobile library in 1951

Introduced by Solihull Public Libraries in 1950, the ideal vehicle for the troublesome reader, a mobile library converted from a two-ton prison van

The C.D. mobile library, designed to expand on site to accommodate at least twenty borrowers: 1952. It did not go into production

In 1952 C.D. Productions announced the unique mobile library. It was designed with the help of many librarians and C.D. considered the inadequacy of existing mobiles before planning their own. They used a patented expandable girder method in which the sides of the trailer expanded by a simple mechanism, which produced twice the floor area. The mobile was designed to hold 4,500 books and had ample room for twenty borrowers to circulate. It apparently did not go into production. C.D. had their timing right for the introduction of such a mobile. The financial situation was gradually improving and authorities could begin to consider custom-built vehicles. K.C. Harrison wrote of this period:

"So, for the first time (in the post-war years) mobile libraries which thus far had been seen only in the rural England of A.E. Housman or Edward Thomas, began to show themselves in the Victorian streets of Acton and Battersea, and in the suburban avenues of North London."

During the period K.C. Harrison was writing about, regionalization of library systems was gradually being introduced. Derbyshire had regionalized just before the war and Sheffield just after. Many authorities used mobile library boundaries as guide lines when determining the limits of each region.

By the end of 1952 over one hundred mobile libraries were in service in the United Kingdom and mobile library development was expanding in every part of the world.

1953 saw the introduction to the streets of Woolwich the type of mobile library K.C. Harrison had written about. Designed to provide temporary relief until permanent branch librries could be built, the vehicle was very popular. It called on seven sites with such brisk borrowing that 2,200 new readers were attracted almost immediately and many existing readers deserted permanent branches for the new mobile library. Also in 1953, the rural areas of Anglesey were to be served by the introduction of a mobile library. Its purchase was covered by the Welsh Church Tithe Fund vested in the council. Montgomeryshire in the same year, unable to provide additional mobiles but wishing to expand the service to include a larger area, changed from a two to three-week cycle visit. In April 1954 D.A. South of Derbyshire County Library commented that more than eighty mobile libraries had been

Nottinghamshire mobile library, 1952

Most of the Essex fleet of mobile libraries and exhibition vans, 1955

introduced during the last few years serving rural areas, and that traditional thinking about the provision of a library service in a specific area was obsolete where mobile libraries were concerned. The theory concerning maximum distances which a reader could be expected to travel to a library was urban thinking totally inapplicable in rural terms. Derbyshire County Library realized it was out of the question to serve every reader in the County. Choosing the standard Bedford vehicle which had limitations off reasonable roads meant at least 250 people in Derbyshire would be outside the mobile library service.

Derbyshire was the first county to admit that a door-to-door library service in the county was not possible.

In 1954 Sunderland introduced its first mobile library and Lancashire its eleventh. During the same year a survey carried out among the seventeen urban authorities in London and the Home Counties with mobile libraries revealed that fourteen of them regarded mobiles as a permanent feature of their service.

By 1954 the Family Book Service was introduced by the Librarian of the Orkney Islands to serve the twenty five smaller islands. A mobile library service and village centres were impractical so each family was sent on request a collection of books, usually 12 to 16, which could be retained for up to two months. They were delivered by steamer and then by local traders' vans. The number of books issued increased from 4,000 a year to nearly 58,000.

By 1955 mobile library provision seemed to be established. Forty-nine counties had 141 mobile libraries among them and only fifteen counties seemed reluctant to introduce them. The West Riding of Yorkshire Library with twenty vehicles had no fewer than 3,467 travelling library stops in the year 1954/5.

Radnorshire County Library mobile

*The first mobile library in Wales which offered a continuous direct service.
Operating until 1960, when it was sold to a local trader, it vanished into the
Borth bog during the late sixties, this photograph shows it as a Cardiganshire
Joint Library mobile library operating in the north of the county.*

Despite such developments, library centres still existed in their
thousands, two-thirds of them in schools with all the obvious
disadvantages.

During the mid fifties mobile libraries were so much a part of
the library establishment that when Sheila Bannister wrote in
the *Assistant Librarian:*
"the ideal mobile librarian needs to know as much about motor
mechanics as librarianship "
many mobile librarians must have known exactly what Miss
Bannister meant. The practical problems of the mobile
librarian were expressed in her article, including the difficulties
of enforcing rigid rules that were operational in a branch library
but difficult to enforce on a mobile library because of the
personal relationship that builds up between reader and mobile

librarian. It was during this period that the myth of mobile library work developed. Ideas generated about a leisurely brand of librarianship associated with warm countryside and numerous cups of tea from grateful readers. In fact little could be further from the truth. B. Oliph Smith probably sized up mobile librarianship most accurately, pointing out in 1949 that the mobile librarian needed a:

"certain hardiness of body".

The myth should have been exploded for ever in 1957 when the pages of the *Assistant Librarian* bristled with correspondence after a letter that requested comment from mobile librarians: "Let's hear from the travelling librarians; a honk or hoot would be enough".

Different views on issuing systems, even names for mobile librarians were soon apparent. Such comments as:

"I am old-fashioned enough to believe that little things such as calling a mobile library a van do matter. Little things such as this, and calling one's driver by his Christian name, wearing slacks or plunging necklines lead eventually to slack and slapdash in larger issues."

produced spirited replies for several months.

The following year more heated correspondence hit the pages of the *Assistant Librarian,* this time on the terminology for a library on wheels: Mobile Library, Travelling Van, Book-mobile, Bibliobus and Bookbus were just some of the titles.

As mobile libraries improved in design, conditions for the staff gradually improved. Netherton, one of the Bootle housing estates, had a mobile library holding 3,000 books plus an all-electric kitchenette for the staff. Wiltshire introduced a second mobile library based at Marlborough, equipped with a basin and hot water for the staff. It was described as:

"probably the most modern in the West of England".

Mobile libraries had frequently caught the attention of the media and in February 1958 the BBC featured a short film about the inauguration of a mobile library service in Surrey. Advances continued to be made in design and used for mobile libraries, but not everyone welcomed a rapid development in mobile library provision.

In 1958 a proposal to spend £2,000 on launching a mobile library service in the Isle of Ely was considered by an alderman on the education committee to be:

"another nail in the coffin of village life".

He felt that library vans killed the spirit of village life and that the existing centres provided adequate and free service for those with a thirst for education and literature.

A vehicle was eventually purchased and readers did not have to wait as long for a library service as did their cousins in West Suffolk. The County Librarian of West Suffolk had to fight a ten-year campaign before approval was given for the introduction of a mobile library into a predominantly rural county. The struggle started in December 1948 when a report was presented to the Education Committee of West Suffolk County Council on the desirability of the introduction of a 25-30 cwt van costing £340 plus annual running costs of about £600 to supply the reading needs of 33 parishes without a library centre. This was rejected because of the high cost and the probable small benefits which might arise! Three years later another report went forward giving details of mobile library developments in other parts of the country plus increased costs to supply the same service. It was hoped to introduce the service by April, 1953. In July, 1955 West Suffolk County rejected another plan to introduce a mobile library service. The storm in council raged around the proposal to employ a driver for the vehicle as well as a librarian. One councillor thought the scheme excellent but did not see why the librarian did not drive himself. Another felt if the scheme were approved:
"We shall soon have a man to drive the milkman around".
By four votes the scheme was referred back to the Education Committee for consideration. However, ten years after the introduction of the original report, West Suffolk County Library took delivery of the first mobile library. But the ratepayers had the last word, a letter in the local paper deplored the introduction of the mobile and regretted the closing of the centres.

Such opposition was by no means restricted to the eastern counties but nevertheless mobile libraries increased in number. Pressures at mobile library stops soon became the guidance for branch library provision. New thinking continued and discussions on trailer as opposed to self propelled mobile libraries continued. Trailer libraries were an asset in built up urban areas, acting as a mobile branch library. But were of limited value in a rural area. Luton Public Libraries hoped to convince those who doubted the value of trailers by pointing out that two trailers are only slightly more expensive than one self-propelled mobile.

Towards the end of 1959, an article by Miss S Hamilton appeared in the *Yorkshire Post,* that described her job as a mobile librarian with the West Riding County Library:
"I am immune to surprises. The last time we went out we had to rescue a cow that had its head trapped between the bars of a gate."

Bootle Public Libraries, December 1958

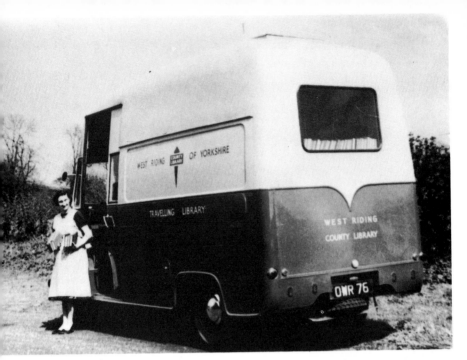

West Riding County Library: smallest vehicle for door-to-door service

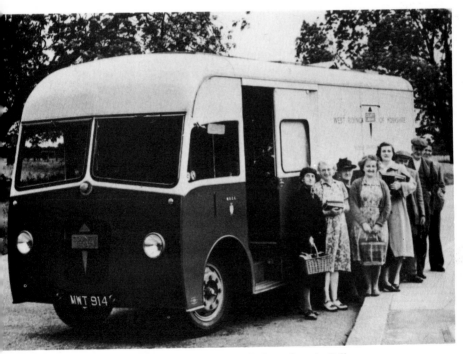

West Riding County Library: Intermediate vehicle used in the Selby area

5. The Years of Local Government Re-organisation

During the early nineteen-sixties successive governments had felt that the shifting population changes that occurred during the post-war years meant that local government boundaries and administrative machinery needed amending. So over a ten-year period, beginning in 1965, virtually every part of the United Kingdom saw changes in local government boundaries and responsibilities. These changes coincided with the final phase of mobile library introduction. In the early nineteen-sixties the village centre was being rapidly phased out as all progressive authorities continued to build up their mobile library fleets. The village centre, in the majority of cases, was already a moribund institution and statistical evidence tended to support this view. By 1960 the County Librarian of Hampshire was pointing out that when a mobile library was introduced to replace a village centre in Hampshire borrowing increased four to five times. Similar figures had been reported by B. O. Smith about the West Riding village centres back in the late forties. With these figures in mind, Hampshire made plans for the future with fourteen mobiles proposed for communites of between 2,000 and 6,000 and full time branches for over 6,000; opening hours to be determined by catchment area served.

1960 was an excellent year for mobile library expansion. Brecon introduced its first, while Carlisle's first mobile attracted nearly one thousand new readers in the first four weeks. Hungary also introduced her first mobile libraries. The main difference between the mobile libraries of Hungary and the United Kingdom is that the Hungarian vehicles tend to show films after book selection and grateful readers usually give the staff flowers.

Grateful readers are part of the mobile library tradition. The staff on Cornwall's new mobile based on Bodmin were given a crate of broccoli in appreciation of supplying "a light one for the wife." Grateful readers were also featured during a film

Watford Public Libraries trailer library with Scammell towing unit 1961

Once an authority had arrived at a design that appeared to eliminate many of these problems, they were obviously reluctant to change from it.

Early in 1961 Dumfries County Library introduced its first mobile library. At that time there were fifteen other mobile libraries operating in Scotland. The first Dumfries vehicle was on an Austin chassis, a 303, extended to 24 ft to carry a stock of 2,300 volumes. During its first year of operation 9,617 miles were covered on 224 journeys and a total of 63,104 books were issued to 1,757 borrowers. Another new development in Scotland was the introduction by Lanarkshire County Library of a £3,000 mobile library to replace fifty village centres.

Meanwhile, in the Principality maximum use was made of Caernarvonshire's mobile library. Likewise introduced in 1961, the vehicle provided a monthly book supply to all branch libraries plus a termly book supply to every school in the County. During the same year Hertfordshire made another film about mobile libraries, this time for showing in the Middle East.

Although the advantages of purpose-built over converted vehicles had become apparent by the early sixties, not every authority could afford the luxury of purpose-built mobile libraries. Sheffield was one such authority who introduced a single-decker bus as a mobile library in the summer of 1962, to serve areas of the city affected by the closure of 117 library centres. At the same time readers visited by a Dorset county mobile library were told they could borrow as many books as they could read in a fortnight. Hearing this an old colonel came along with a wheel barrow and took out 56 books! The Dorset colonel was just one of the many readers served by the 338 mobiles operated by library authorities in the United Kingdom during the summer of 1962.

Despite the steady increase in numbers of mobile libraries put into service (Hampshire alone added four in 1962); not all authorities were instantly convinced that mobile libraries were the answer to village centres. West Sussex County Library first carried out a pilot scheme, beginning in December 1959, to test the validity of mobile libraries. Selected areas in West Sussex were visited by a mobile library one day per fortnight; the rest of the time the vehicle changed the stock in village centres throughout the County. Two years after the introduction of the pilot scheme the mobile library was serving over 350 readers with an average issue of 750 per visit. As a result of this evidence mobile libraries were gradually to be introduced eventually replacing all village centres.

Towards the end of 1962 the Working Party on Standards of Public Library Service in England and Wales under the Chairmanship of H. T. Bourdillon, reported their findings. The Working Party reported on most aspects of library services. They considered that many questions relating to mobile library services needed further examination.

By mid-1963 there were 337 mobile libraries serving more than three million readers through 150 public library authorities in the U.K. During the same year a mobile library rally had been organized as a special feature of the Joint Conference of Northern Branches of the Library Association at Blackpool. The rally attracted much interest with librarians and public alike.

Earlier in 1963 Moray County Library introduced a mobile library exclusively for primary school children. Holding 2,000 books, it offered accommodation for thirty-six pupils, their teacher and library staff. Schools were to be visited fortnightly and each class was allowed twenty minutes to select books. Not all authorities were as progressive as Moray and as one might expect, mobile library development for young people varied enormously.

A Library Association survey carried out in 1954 revealed that of 468 authorities which completed the questionnaire only 10% had mobile libraries carrying children's stock. The situation had improved somewhat five years later, though in Scotland only Aberdeen Public Libraries had a mobile library with services to children. By the late 'fifties the problems of public libraries within school buildings that closed during

The largest mobile library operated by the West Riding of Yorkshire County Library: March 1963

school vacations were becoming apparent.

In 1958 Nottinghamshire introduced the first summer-holiday mobile library service with two vehicles being used. Each was staffed by a children's librarian and visited sixteen villages. By the late 'sixties this service had expanded into visits to one hundred villages. Shropshire and Wiltshire introduced similar services in 1966. The Wiltshire service was started first to an RAF station at Colerne where each week approximately 260 children borrowed over 2,000 books. The following year the service was increased to five areas of the County and catered for children up to the age of fourteen years. The summer-holiday mobile library service gradually grew until the majority of authorities offered something similar. By 1970 all county libraries with the exception of East Sussex operated mobile libraries, but many included books for pre-school children only, as opposed to young people. Many of the problems concerning mobile libraries and provision of material for young people have yet to be settled.

In 1963 the County Libraries Group of the Library Association produced a *Policy survey of the county libraries of the U.K., 1951 to 1961*. The forty-one English counties that completed the survey revealed some interesting statistics. During the period concerned the number of mobile libraries increased from 66 to 199 while the number of library centres fell from 9,160 to 4,827. In Northern Ireland no mobile libraries were in operation during 1951, ten years later eight were in service. The returns from Scotland were disappointing with replies from only 19 out of 30 counties complete, and only 4 out of the 19 gave details of any mobile library provision. Attitudes towards mobile library coverage in the Scottish counties differed; one

Anglesey mobile library built by Stevens Bros of Fleet

librarian stated that in a county scattered with isolated pockets of population a mobile library could not be justified. While another held the same view but felt the answer lay in the post possible postal service. An extension of this attitude was reflected several times in the report. But the situation in Scotland was definitely changing. C. S. Minto toured the northern counties of Scotland in 1964, something he had last done in 1948. He was able to report to the Scottish Library Association that all but two of the nine counties involved in the survey were either operating or planning a mobile library service.

Conditions in Scotland could be desolate and the mobile library was frequently at the mercy of the weather. In Sutherland a bookmobile served the scattered hamlets and farmsteads with a three-weekly service returning to its base at weekends. Once, during a particularly bad snowstorm it was standed at an inn for two weeks!

During July, 1964, the Public Libraries and Museums Act became law. As well as being the most important library legislation since 1919 the Public Libraries and Museums Act repealed all previous library legislation. Although the Act was very important in terms of library provision it had little to add on the subject of mobile libraries. By 1965 many of the problems encountered by mobile librarians were coming to the fore: professional isolation, limited stock, often very uncomfortable working conditions and many more. The previous year an alarm bell and light signal were fitted to Hornsey's mobile library in case of rowdyism at the more isolated sites. Other authorities began to introduce similar measures such as radios, alarms, police calls or allowing only male staff to work on the vehicles.

Perhaps with some of these problems in mind, Mr. A. D. Mortimore and five colleagues on the staff of Gloucestershire County Library stated in the September 1965 edition of the Library Association Record that they proposed asking the Council of the Library Association to create a Branch and Mobile Libraries Section to unite all those engaged in, or interested in, this field of librarianship. Mr. Mortimore appealed for names to go forward to the Library Association to support the proposed group. Ninety-two members sent in

Wiltshire County Library Holiday Mobile Scheme, 1966. The scheme was started at an RAF station and gradually expanded throughout the county

Gloucester County School Library Service mobile, built by Booker Motor Bodies Ltd of Devon

names and the Council authorized the formation of the new group in December 1965.

During 1965 Mr. C. R. Eastwood, already the foremost authority on mobile library provision in the United Kingdom had written:
"In the future mobile accommodation will be no less comfortable and appropriate than in the best static library."

In the late 'sixties the development of mobile libraries was steady and even occasionally spectacular. As a result of local government reorganization, Northampton extended its boundaries in April 1965. A mobile library was introduced to serve the additional area. The vehicle issued almost a quarter of a million books in one year. During the evenings it was common to have more staff on the mobile than in the central library.

During 1966 East Suffolk decided over a period of years to replace its 137 branch libraries by mobile libraries. Many of these branch libraries were village centres often open for only an hour or two a fortnight; while in the same year Midhurst, West Sussex introduced a new mobile library specially designed for the narrow roads in the area.

As was characteristic of many large urban systems, Nottingham Public Libraries did not introduce a mobile library until 1967, when the library service in the city had been established almost one hundred years. Branch library development until the last war had covered the inner areas of the city and twenty years of post-war building took care of the rest of the city. The mobile library was introduced to serve the areas that did not justify a branch library but needed a library service.

It was the unlikely factors that influenced the number of books issued by some Welsh mobile libraries during 1967. Montgomeryshire lost some 20,000 issues through bad weather plus foot and mouth disease that restricted vehicle movement. Further west, issue figures were affected during National Library Week, when the staff of Cardiganshire Joint Library used the narrow gauge railway to carry books between Aberystwyth and Devils Bridge. Villages in the Rheidol Valley were normally served by mobile libraries, but to celebrate National Library Week books were carried by the train. It stopped at each village and readers were invited to select books directly from the train. The BBC filmed the event and all but a handful of books were borrowed. An example of British Rail operating a mobile library!

In 1967 car ownership and public library use was an engaging subject. Questions on the value of mobile libraries in an apparently car-orientated society came to the fore. Few really felt that car ownership would reduce the importance of mobile libraries; limitations of personal finance, physical and social handicaps, problems with town centre access made mobile library provision more desirable. And that was in the days when petrol cost 23p a gallon. Correspondence about the design faults of mobile libraries had appeared in the professional press for over a decade. Blame for design and faults was placed on Chief Librarians who had forgotten what a book was like, technical departments of local authorities and mobile library builders. The Branch and Mobile Libraries Group of the Library Association held a one-day school on the subject in 1967 when representatives of all interested parties were asked to put forth views.

During 1967 two books on mobile libraries were published: C. R. Eastwood's *Mobile Libraries and other Public Library Transport* published by the Association of Assistant Librarians, essentially a look at British mobile development; and E. F. Brown's "Bookmobiles and Bookmobile Service" published by the Scarecrow Press, a comprehensive account of mobile libraries in the USA and Canada. Mr. Brown's book includes such un-British habits as dressing up the bookmobile for a Christmas parade, organizing a "Name the Bookmobile" contest and included details of a "package deal bookmobile" or supplying a trailer complete with all accessories, charging equipment, catalogues, books ready processed and catalogued for the shelves. Mr. Eastwood's book has remained the textbook on the subject dealing with the development of mobile libraries in all parts of the world, though written principally from the English county point of view.

That few county librarians were treating mobile libraries as branch libraries on wheels was evident from some statistics produced by the Society of County Librarians early in 1968. Of the 56 counties that replied to the section on details of fines and charges, 43 did not charge fines on mobile libraries. Of the remaining 13, 11 applied the same rate as branch libraries and 2 applied a reduced scale.

Another survey that produced some interesting statistics relevant to mobile libraries was carried out in 1968 by the Association of Assistant Librarians. The survey requested

Ealing Public Libraries mobile library built by G. C. Smith

Built by G. C. Smith for Wolverhampton Public Libraries in 1967. Sold ten years later, now a mobile boutique in the West Country

Some of the changes in trailer library design

Hartlepool Public Libraries mobile library introduced 1971

information about working conditions in libraries. Of the 141 authorities that provided information about mobile libraries, 10 per cent provided toilet facilities, 43 per cent provided washing facilities and 33 per cent provided lunch stops, usually coinciding with visits to school. Authorities were clearly recognising the desirability of providing washing and toilet facilities on mobile libraries but the additional costs made them a luxury and not a necessity.

By the April of 1970, 540 mobile libraries were operating throughout the U.K. and the importance of this branch of the

75

library profession was now evident. The 1971 publication from the Department of Education and Science, "Public Library Service Points" stated that mobile libraries provided the most satisfactory means of bringing library facilities to communities of less than 1,500 population, including scattered hamlets and isolated farms. A minimum halt of about 15 minutes was desirable even in the most isolated stop. On the basis of fortnightly visits the population served by a single mobile library could seldom be expected to exceed 12,000 and might be considerably less in sparsely populated areas. The latest mobile to go into service in 1972 was a helicopter flying out from Lindsey and Holland County Library at Louth, Lincolnshire, to engineers working on the North Sea Gas offshore platform east of Mablethorpe.

During 1973, as the legislation and planning of local government reorganizations went ahead, complaints from staff working on mobile libraries poured forth. Complaints ranged from working in summer temperatures of up to 110 degrees or in outdoor clothing during winter. A complaint about the lack of washing facilities on the mobile library in one authority were rewarded by offers of an enamel bowl and a thermos flask of hot water. Despite complaints the more progressive authorities were already consulting the staff who worked on the vehicles when re-designing mobile libraries or trailers. However, in some authorities staff worked in conditions little better than those on the horse and cart in Warrington over a century earlier.

The 1973 publication from the Department of Education and Science: *The public library service: re-organization and after,* offered guidance to librarians in the immediate post reorganization period. On the subject of mobile library provision the D.E.S. commented:

"In a number of cases the larger size of administrative units will make it economically feasible for the first time to extend mobile services to cover pockets of population, particularly on the outskirts of towns, which are at present served, if at all, by small inadequate service points."

or,

"whenever it enables the maintenance of a more efficient service, adjoining authorities should make whatever mutual arrangements seem necessary to them to permit mobile libraries to operate across administrative boundaries."

The latter piece of advice had already been taken by the London Boroughs of Brent and Harrow who as a result of the 1965 reorganization of London boroughs had agreed to share a mobile library operating across borough boundaries.

So in 1974 an opportunity was available for library services to gain the maximum from their mobile libraries.

Borough of Bilston

Mobile Library Service

The Mobile Library service is planned to bring books to you. About 2,000 can be carried on the vehicle at one time. These will be changed regularly so that you will always be able to find fresh reading. The Mobile Library cannot offer you the same selection as the library in Mount Pleasant, which has over 34,000 books. But the staff of the Mobile Library will make full use of all the books owned by Bilston to meet your reasonable needs. Any book in either library can be "Reserved" for you on payment of a fee, at present threepence, and you will be notified when the book is ready to be collected.

Your library ticket can be used at either library. You do NOT need to join twice. To obtain library tickets it is necessary to fill in a joining card. If you are over the age of twenty-one and live in Bilston, all we need is your full name and address in ordinary hand-writing. If you are not yet twenty-one or do not live in Bilston, we shall ask you to obtain the additional signature of a Bilston resident who is over twenty-one, a Householder or Elector.

Books are loaned for a period of fourteen days and must be returned on or before the last date stamped on the date label. This loan can be renewed upon request, provided that the book is not in demand by another library member. When renewing a loan you must produce either the book or a note of the number appearing on the pocket inside the front cover and the date on which the book was due for return.

If books are kept longer than the loan period without being renewed, fines are charged. These fines run at one penny for the first week or part week overdue, then at threepence for every following week or part week. A book overdue by eight days carries a fine of fourpence.

The places and times of the Mobile Library service are set out below. We look forward to helping you with your work at home, in the factory, the office, at school—or to helping you just forget it all.

Yours faithfully,

Alderman MISS A. FELLOWS,
Chairman of Committee.

TIMETABLE

The Mobile Library service will start on the afternoon of Tuesday, 1st March, 1960.

	MORNING 10—12.30	AFTERNOON 2.15—5.0 : 5.30—6.45
TUESDAY	ST. CHAD'S ROAD	JORDAN PLACE
WEDNESDAY	HARDY SQUARE	JEAVON PLACE
THURSDAY	PRINCESS SQUARE	JOHN STREET
FRIDAY	OAKLANDS GREEN	VILLIERS SQUARE

The mobile library is coming

Two mobile libraries introduced within a ten-year period. Nottingham Public Libraries vehicle in 1967, top, whilst, below, a modern Nottinghamshire vehicle. Few basic changes in design

6. An Opportunity

The reorganization of local government during the decade 1965-1975 reduced the number of library authorities from 506 at the beginning of the decade to 161 at its close.

Virtually all parts of the United Kingdom were affected by changes. These changes in local government boundaries and responsibilities created more problems than will ever get into print but they did provide mobile libraries with additional challenges.

The reorganizations involving London, the West Midlands and Teesside were a mixed blessing in terms of mobile library provision. Essentially changes involving urban areas, they usually expanded at the expense of county library services, frequently taking in county mobile libraries in the process. County mobiles were often bought for rural use and new authorities using rural mobile libraries in an urban situation did not always create the best service. But as the new authorities established themselves and replacement vehicles were ordered the service rapidly improved.

The major reorganizations affecting England, Wales and Scotland in 1974 and 1975 respectively created greater challenge for mobile library innovators. Traditional innovators in mobile library provision like the West Riding of Yorkshire and Lanark vanished overnight to be replaced by population units that varied in size from Hampshire (1,500,000) to Bearsden and Milngavie (population 37,000); or with a readership density like that of the Highland Region with 0.1 density of population per hectare to Liverpool with 48 per hectare.

From the point of view of library organisation the creation of larger units in terms of population and square miles to be covered provided a golden opportunity for the use of mobile libraries. It made more effective use of mobile libraries possible, right across the county authorities and to operate in areas previously overlooked owing to the difficulties of route planning around some static service points.

Hertfordshire became just one authority that was able to gain the maximum from her six rural and eight urban trailers to provide a truly county-wide mobile library service.

Mobile libraries really had an opportunity to come into their own serving the scattered readership within some of the newly formed large yet sparsely populated authorities. The new Welsh county of Gwynedd had problems serving a population the size of Barnsley spread over an area of 1,500 square miles. Mobile libraries were the only way to provide any sort of library service. Seven mobile libraries served the area, normally fortnightly but monthly to the more isolated areas. In a county with many second homes and a seasonal fluctuating population, the service had to be adjusted to take account of these changes. To have built static service points to cope with such a wide-spread dispersed population was for Gwynedd a financial impossibility. In 1975 the service was described as being overworked, with not enough professional expertise, too little contact being made with rural library users, but apparently coping.

Similar problems were produced as a result of the 1975 reorganization of local authorities in Scotland when the country was redivided into nine regions and three island areas. In the Grampian Region of Scotland three of the district authorities amalgamated in 1975 to form the North-East of Scotland Library Service. Operating a service to a population of 160,000 usually in some communities over an area of 2,500 square miles offers a challenge to any librarian. Again mobile libraries were the only economic way the area could have a library service. Eight vehicles operate over the region. The five that cover the least populated areas are one-man operated. Qualified librarians are not employed on the vehicles, as the authority felt that cost-effectiveness ruled this out. The smaller vehicles carry 2,000 books plus several hundred records and a small selection of framed prints. No fines, fees or charges are made, no receipt books are kept, one ticket is used per family and, in theory, all disagreements with readers are avoided. All parts of the area are served by the mobile library network and the only reasons the mobiles do not operate is driver's sickness or mechanical problems. In Scotland the North-East of Scotland Library Service's problems are not unique. The Dumfries and

80

Galloway Region Library Service serves a population of 143,000 spread over 2,500 square miles, again making maximum use of mobile libraries.

Urban areas were also radically affected by reorganizations often offering new opportunities for mobile library provision. As a result of the 1974 Local Government Reorganization the boundaries of the City of Coventry expanded to include semi-rural parishes previously administered by Warwickshire County Library mobile library.

Coventry decided to obtain a mobile library with the primary object of serving these semi-rural areas but also to provide a service to areas of the city remote from a full time branch library. The vehicle, which went into service in March, 1975 is based on a Ford R104 chassis and is 32ft long, 10ft 6ins high and 8ft wide. With a Webasto battery-powered heating system and a fan for use in warm weather it aimed at maximum comfort for staff and reader. Additional comfort for the staff includes a small kitchen and toilet unit. It was not felt justified that a qualified librarian need man the vehicle but two interesting developments assist staffing.

The issue system is a Plessey Light Pen through a Portable Data Capture Unit on the vehicle. The issuing and discharging of books are recorded on to cassette tapes which are transferred to the authority's mainframe computer via a converter. This type of issue system had first been introduced on to a mobile library by Solihull Public Libraries when their new mobile library went into service early in 1975. Computer charging is just one of many issuing systems in use on mobile libraries but as computerisation within libraries grows it is obviously the charging system for the mobile libraries of the future.

Another interesting development within the Coventry mobile library is the introduction of a Radiophone, a service operated by the Post Office, that enables a call to be made or received from any telephone in the country. Radiotelephones within mobile libraries are not unique to Coventry. Hertfordshire and several other authorities introduced them during the middle sixties, usually to urban vehicles that had problems of vandalism. But in Coventry the Radiophone is a vital part of the service, not to be regarded for emergency use only. The radiotelephone enables the assistant to have the total resources

Mobile library meetings are an opportunity for vehicles to be displayed and for mobile librarians to discuss common problems and topical issues. Mobile 76 was organized by the Scottish AAL

Solihull introduced this mobile library early in 1975. With a Plessey Light Pen charging system, toilet and washing facilities, it was, when introduced, the most advanced mobile library in operation. Built by Hind of Carlisle.

of the Coventry City Libraries, Arts and Museums Department at the push of a button. Local government reorganization invariably made authorities examine their changed service once this was possible. Reports were generated and many internal investigations were carried out in which the role of the mobile library was reconsidered. The value of mobile libraries to both rural and urban communities had been demonstrated during the previous two decades and many attempts were made to replace older vehicles or expand mobile library fleets. Unfortunately the changes and need to expand coincided with economic gloom and rethinking about mobile library expansion had to be shelved.

Even those authorities who qualified for urban aid could not always obtain the funding to introduce new conventional mobile libraries. So converted vehicles began to appear on the streets again. But this time they were aimed at one group of readers — children. From the Warrington vehicle onwards mobile libraries have attracted children. Realising this, several authorities began to introduce converted double-decker buses or specially built mobile libraries aimed at children. The vehicles usually had only one thing in common: they were eye catching. Leicester County Libraries introduced a magic mobile library into the supposedly non-reading areas of Leicester during the summer of 1975. The vehicle, a converted double-decker corporation bus decorated with witches, goblins and ghosts was undoubtedly eye-catching. Aiming a programme at the under fourteens and their parents, it involved films, competitions and storytimes. With stops of around one hour over 9,000 children visited the bus in six weeks. Hampshire County Library introduced a pink Book Bus into Southampton during late 1975. The vehicle had more than a community liaison role to play. The librarian, who has a responsibility for using the vehicle to break down the barriers that static libraries create for children, described herself as a combination of social worker, nanny, community relations worker, teacher and librarian, but not necessarily in that order!

Many authorities have used similar ideas. The London Borough of Hammersmith's mobile library for children aptly called *The Pied Piper* was introduced in the summer of 1975. Painted flamingo pink with a dancing Pied Piper motif in dark blue, the mobile library visits eighteen schools where access to normal library facilities is difficult. During the school holidays the vehicle operates for children of all ages, when it parks on a regular basis as near to their schools as possible.

The following year Shropshire County Library introduced their own Pied Piper mobile library to the Telford New Town area. Using a vehicle that looked more like an ice cream van than a mobile library with such informal ideas as books stored in barrels, the vehicle has proved to be very popular.

Ideas to gain more from mobile libraries poured forth — design, fuels, charging systems staffing and publicity. The simplest publicity ideas seemed to work best like advertising mobile route changes on local radio or painting 'mobile library' on the roof of a vehicle so that potential readers in high rise flats can see that a mobile library and not a removal vehicle has arrived.

The middle 'seventies were another age of converting vehicles, mostly from the point of view of economics, but also because some converted vehicles appeared to do the job as well as purpose-built. Double-decker buses similar to the type introduced by Leicester and Southampton were also introduced by Newcastle-upon-Tyne to serve all parts of the borough while Derbyshire County Library introduced a double-decker bus to serve most parts of the County. The bus, converted at a cost of £5,300 is a far cry from the converted vehicles of the immediate post war years that became mobile libraries often for under £20. It is interesting to note that many librarians had advocated for years that double-decker buses would make ideal mobile libraries particularly serving urban areas. With sensible conversion and a paperback stock on the upper deck they would hold far more stock than a conventional mobile library. But when double-deckers have been converted to mobile libraries they have been used almost exclusively for work with young people.

Despite the most rapid developments in mobile library design and use, many village centres still remain, though they are on the decline. After some consideration West Sussex County Library announced early in 1976 that village centres within the County would eventually be closed and where necessary replaced by the mobile library. The County Librarian added:

"Experience shows that the mobile library gives a far better selection of books to a community, attracts borrowers from a wider cross-section of the population and issues more books than a static village centre."

LIBRARIES, INFORMATION AND LOCAL STUDIES

Books are lent from the Central Lending Library, a Mobile Library, and a network of 11 full-time branches and ten part-time library centres.

For those unable to visit a library, a Housebound Readers Service exists in certain parts of the City, and library services are provided on-site, for staff and patients at the Walsgrave Hospital.

Book loans are free to all who live, work or attend full-time educational establishments in the City. Books not available from the stock of the City Libraries may be borrowed on behalf of readers from libraries at home and abroad.

This is your Library Service

Lincolnshire Library Service

Thirteen mobile libraries serve the rural areas, travelling over 127,200 miles each year and visiting 2,219 stops each fort-night. A typical day varies considerably with as many as 44 stops around the Holland area to as few as four in Tattershall.

7. The Future

The future of mobile libraries has frequently been in doubt. Challenged by virtually everything from prices of fuel and vehicles, a car owning society that would not need mobile libraries, adequate branch libraries and a decline in rural users, but new ideas with mobile libraries have always poured forth, some definitely unworkable while others are perhaps the answer to some of the problems. Bradford Public Libraries, innovators in many areas, introduced travelling libraries in 1902 and closed the last one early in 1977. They are now experimenting with 'Transportable Libraries'. The transportable library consists of shelving units with fixed wheels plus a transportable counter and kinder box. The units are transported from one building to another. The first library was opened in Willesden in June of 1976 and issued about 1000 books a week. The book stock exceeds 4,000 volumes and the library is open two days a week. The scheme is being expanded because it offers many benefits. A conventional vehicle is used to transport the shelving at the beginning of each day thus freeing the vehicle for deliveries during the rest of the day. No huge amounts of stock are tied up in centres used only a few days a week. A branch library is established meeting a demand that will probably fluctuate. If sufficient pressure is applied to the part-time transportable library then additional opening hours can be arranged. It is a system cheaper and more flexible than village centre or conventional branch library. Finances have been the governing factor throughout the 'seventies and many of the changes introduced to mobile library services were dictated by economic pressures.

After an investigation by Paul Turner of Derbyshire County Library on the mobile library service in his county, thinking about the provision of new mobile library vehicles changed. As a result early in 1977 a 'container' library was introduced. The change was to use a commercial container as a mobile library. The container is similar to those used on lorry trailers for exporting goods all over the world. The container is transported to sites and it can be parked for a number of days, where it can be sealed and left overnight. Using a York semi-drop deck freightmaster measuring 40' long by 8' wide the container will hold up to 5,000 books with a life span of up to 20 years. The container has an adult lending section, separate junior library, plus a small staff kitchen and toilets. Its additional advantages are that it is virtually vandal-proof and at £12,000 is considered better value than a conventional trailer.

Container libraries are not a new concept. Shropshire County Library had investigated the possibilities of using them but they were first introduced by Cornwall County Library in 1972. Prior to the introduction of containers Cornwall had nine mobile libraries which accounted for 36% of all books loaned in the County using a basic 20% of the County bookstock. It was the policy to provide branch libraries in centres of 3,000-plus population and serve the surrounding area of each branch with a mobile library. However it was felt that sixty communities needed a better service than a mobile library could offer but financial limits made branch library building in all required areas impossible. The container was deemed the intermediate solution. Containers hold up to 6,000 books in 300 sq. ft. units and are taken to each site by a tractor and trailer from which the container is side loaded on to a prepared site, usually a car park, where it is left for 48 hours and open to the public for 18 hours during that period. Transference of containers usually takes place at night. But problems with siting, the Cornish roads and difficulties with spare parts for the towing unit created a situation that made the service gradually more and more unreliable. Eventually the container service will be discontinued, the containers becoming branch libraries on a permanent site and other arrangements introduced for the remaining sites.

The energy crisis of the middle 'seventies hit internal combustion engines the world over. Mobile libraries were affected immediately, petrol engines offering a poorer return than diesel. Authorities had to provide additional income to meet the unforeseen increase in fuel prices. This resulted in reduced routes, reduced frequency of visits and a search for a cheaper fuel.

In this country several authorities investigated the use of Liquefied Petroleum Gas as an experimental fuel. Liquefied Petroleum Gas, L.P.G. for short, was first introduced in Bradford and Norwich. L.P.G. is a hydrocarbon derived from the refining of crude oil and generally consists of propane or butane which can be liquefied at relatively low temperatures, but will vaporise at normal temperatures. The low price of L.P.G. as compared with petrol is due almost entirely to the lower tax rates and this is a situation which may not be kept if the use of L.P.G. for vehicles increases.

Norfolk County Library have pioneered the use of L.P.G. as a fuel for mobile libraries.

Early in August 1979 Cambridgeshire County Library introduced a mobile library powered by the ultimate in cheap fuels, electricity. The electric mobile proceeds at 12½ m.p.h. around the streets of Cambridge. The vehicle built in Holland is initially expensive, but with a third of the running costs of a conventional mobile library should save £9,000 over a ten-year period.

Despite advances in design and fuel the aim of the service is still much the same as the horse and cart in Warrington. The aim of the service is still to get books to the reader. But what of the person without whom this would not be possible, the mobile library driver? The day has gone when knowledge of horses was an essential qualification to operate a mobile library but conditions for drivers are far from standard. Rates of pay, conditions of services and even titles vary from authority to authority. Some are drivers, others driver/librarian or driver/handyman, mobile library driver assistant, and the list is endless. Conditions of services vary according to location of authority and terrain normally encountered. For example Northumberland provides drivers with uniforms while North Yorkshire provided personnel with smocks and wellington boots. Recruitment difficulties were prevalent in many authorities; demanding a similar licence to industrial drivers and yet not paying a similar salary obviously creates problems. The economic climate and apparent security of local government has helped combat these problems. The delegation of decision-making to drivers also varies. In Bedfordshire it is his decision as to whether service should be discontinued in bad weather or not, while in Cornwall he can assist the public with book selection.

Successive governments have introduced legislation affecting mobile libraries and their drivers. The most relevant recent legislation is the Road Traffic (Drivers' Ages and Hours of Work) Act, 1976, Drivers' Hours (Keeping of Records) Regulations S.I. 1976 and Regulation 543/69 on Drivers' Hours — Derogation.

Mobile libraries continue to be the ideal publicity machine for any local authority. Lincolnshire Library Services' thirteen mobile libraries serve most of the County travelling almost 130,000 miles each year and visiting 2,219 stops each fortnight. A typical day varies considerably with as many as 44 stops around the Holland area to as few as four in Tattershall. Each one advertising the rates in action!

Mobile libraries have tried to move with and ahead of the times through modern fuels, computerisation and the introduction of non-book materials such as pictures, records, posters and cassettes on vehicles. When the paperback revolution finally reached public libraries they seemed the ideal format for mobile libraries. Being more compact and lighter than the conventional hardback book more stock could be placed on vehicles, but few authorities have yet introduced large numbers of paperbacks to their vehicles. The only authority to run an all-paperback stocked mobile library is Dumfries and Galloway.

Mobile libraries are undoubtedly part of the future and so when attempts to remove them are voiced, these are often fiercely resisted. In September 1977 Wiltshire County Council advocated removing Salisbury's mobile library. The cut, which would save £8,410 a year, was attacked as woefully short-sighted by the local Vicar:

"People here are all working class and if the mobile library service is withdrawn it will be yet another nail in the coffin..."

Twenty years previously, a similar argument had been used against the introduction of a mobile library to West Suffolk. During the cuts of the mid-seventies if mobile libraries were threatened it frequently provoked more response than increased fines or Saturday closing; with one West Country Councillor pointing out that the damage caused by depriving children of books through the withdrawal of the mobile library would be out of all proportion to any savings.

But as the economic conditions improve and authorities look to the future, library authorities plan for additional mobile libraries and the introduction of package-deal libraries that are of a mobile type. 'Package-deal' usually means factory-made timber buildings suitable for all purposes including libraries, the better known manufacturers including Vic Hallam, Terrapin and Portakabin. The advantages of these buildings are the speed at which they can be assembled, usually four to six weeks from the site inspection to the issue of the first book. Costs are cheap, often as low as 30% of traditional building costs. Such buildings can be re-used in different parts of the authority similarly to the way containers are used at present.

Mobile libraries in various forms have long provided a service to the housebound. This area will certainly expand in the future. Purpose built housebound mobile libraries are already in use in Hertfordshire and Edinburgh while authorities like the Isle of Wight and Renfrew have purpose-built housebound vehicles with lifts, enabling the physically disabled actually to choose books from the vehicle.

Mobile libraries have come a long way from Warrington and Manchester — they are still moving with the times. That they are capable of doing so is a measure of their effectiveness.

The most recent mobile introduced by Gloucestershire County Library, November 1978

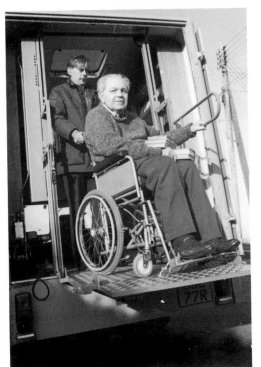

The ultimate in mobile library service to the disabled, a mobile library specially designed to serve housebound readers with a lift for wheelchair access. The vehicle was introduced by the Isle of Wight County Library Service in 1977 with the lift being added in 1978. Since then other library authorities have introduced similar vehicles

91

Dumbarton District Libraries use three mobile libraries to serve 90,000 readers over 200 square miles. Above is an example of the isolated farms that form the bulk of one mobile service

Further Reading

AITKEN, W. R. *History of the Public Library Movement in Scotland.* Scottish Library Association, 1971.

BAKER, E. A. *The Public Library.* Grafton, 1924.

BOWEN, J. and ALLRED, J. *An Investigation into the use and Costs of the Travelling and Part Time Branch Libraries in Oldham.* School of Librarianship, Leeds Polytechnic, 1976.

BRANCH AND MOBILE LIBRARIES GROUP OF THE LIBRARY ASSOCIATION. All publications.

BROWN, J. D. *Manual of Library Economy.* Scott Greenwood, 1903.

CALDWELL, W. *An Introduction to County Library Practice.* A.A.L., 1969.

CARNELL, E. J. *County Libraries.* Grafton, 1938.

CARNEGIE U.K. TRUST. Annual Reports 1913/14 plus. All publications are worth examination.

COOKE, A. S. *County Libraries Manual.* Library Association, 1935.

CORNWALL COUNTY LIBRARY. *Container Libraries.* Cornwall County Library, 1935.

EASTWOOD, C. R. *Mobile Libraries.* A.A.L., 1967.

ELLIS, A. *Library Services for Young People in England and Wales 1830-1970:* Pergamon, 1971.

GREENWOOD, T. *Public Libraries.* Cassell, 1894.

IRWIN, R. *The Origins of the English Library.* Allen and Unwin, 1958.

JOLLIFFE, H. *Public Library Extension Activities.* Library Association, 1968.

KAUFMAN, P. *Libraries and their Users.* Library Association, 1969.

KELLY, T. *Early Public Libraries.* Library Association, 1966.

KELLY, T. *History of Public Libraries in Great Britain 1845-1975.* Library Association, 1977.

LIBRARY TRENDS (3) 9 1961, pp 287-384. An Issue with Details of Mobile Libraries.

LIBRARY ASSOCIATION. *The Years Work in Librarianship:* Library Association, Annually 1929.

McCOLVIN, L. R. *Libraries and the Public:* Allen and Unwin, 1937.

McCOLVIN, L. R. *The Public Library System of Great Britain.* Library Association, 1942.

MINTO, J. *A History of the Public Library Movement in Great Britain and Ireland.* Allen and Unwin, 1932.

MITCHELL, J. M. *The Public Library Systems of Great Britain and Ireland.* Carnegie U.K. Trust, 1924.

MORTIMORE, A. *Branch Libraries.* Deutsch, 1966.

MUNFORD, W. A. *Penny Rate: Aspects of British Public Library History.* Library Association, 1951.

MINFORD, W. A. *James Duff Brown.* Library Association, 1968.

MURISON, W. J. *The Public Library.* Harrap, 1955. 2nd Ed 1971.

OLLE, J. *Library History.* Clive Bingley, 1967.

OSBORNE, E. and SHARR, F. A. *County Library Practice.* Library Association, 1950.

SHARR, F. A. *County Library Transport.* Library Association Pamphlet No 9, 1952.

STOCKHAM, K. A. *British County Libraries 1919-1969.* Deutsch, 1969.

WOOD, B. *A Brief Survey of the Bradford Libraries 1874-1922* Bradford Public Libraries, 1922.

Hammersmith's mobile library called The Pied Piper. *Catering for the 5-11 age group, the library visits 18 schools plus a day nursery. Introduced September 1975*